By the Light of the Silver Moon

Rachel Lister Jones

BookLeaf Publishing

Presentation by *BookLeaf Publishing*

Web: www.bookleafpub.com

E-mail: info@bookleafpub.com

ISBN: 9789357442985

First edition 2023

These poems are dedicated to the other poets in my family- George Leslie Lister, Daphne Lister, Peter Jones, Becky Jones and Jonny Jones.

PREFACE

These poems were all written in 21 days in January and February. They are mainly inspired by the author's walks with her whippet in the deciduous wood over the road from where she lives. Most of the poems are verbal photographs- capturing a moment in time. They are mainly about the connection that the author feels with the natural world.

The Golden Willow Weeps

The golden willow weeps,
Into the mirrored lake.
The tears fall on snow-white swans,
Who glide by gracefully,
In perfect unison,
Whilst a pair of swans, necks entwined,
Declare their mutual eternal love.

The golden willow weeps.
Its tears fall onto the frozen ground,
And turn into the shroud-like bell-flowers,
Of the Virginal snowdrops
Blessed milk-flowers of the snow.
Which spread like a sea of sadness,
Towards the still water

The golden willow weeps,
As the sky turns burnished gold and crimson,
Bathing the swans in golden light.
Then the sky is dark,
Apart from the Snow Moon
Surrounded by a Saint's halo,
As the swans fly into the moonlight.

The Silver Swan

Golden light bathes the silver swan.
The herring- bone sky is reflected in the mirrored lake.
As the sun sets, silhouetted gulls
Cry that another day is ending.
And cormorants shake diamond drops,
From their inky black wings.
The silver swan serenely glides,
Across the lake of pure gold.
A skein of geese fly across the crimson sun,
Flying into the light.
There is a blaze of colour,
Crimson, gold, and burnished orange
Streak across the azure sky,
Then in a blink of an eye, darkness descends.
The last thing I see is the silver swan,
On the cormorant-black lake.

Dawn and Dusk

As dawn breaks,
The silver shroud is removed,
From the wakeful wood.
Night-time hunters,
Wearily return to their nests and dens.
A squirrel stirs in its slumber,
As the sun gradually rises,
Above the horizon, to the East.
There are streaks of gold,
In the moon-silver sky.
The weak Winter sun,
Illuminates the waking wood,
Turning the trees from grey to gold.
Robins and blackbirds sing joyfully,
To proclaim another day dawns.

The hours tick by.
The sun moves in the sky,
But does not warm the earth below.
The dials turn.
Time passes.

It is time to return to the wood.
As we leave the house,
In the West, the sun is setting,

Golden behind a silver herringbone sky,
Turning the wood pink-gold.
As we walk around the wood,
Rooks fly noisily overhead,
On their way back to the roost.
In the warren under the old Ash
Rabbits awaken from forgotten dreams.
A fox stretches in his den.
By the time we are on the far side of the wood,
The sky has changed again.
Leafless trees are silhouetted,
Against a purple-pink sky.
Mackerel clouds obscure the distant hills.
As we leave the park,
The heron-grey shroud,
Is pulled back over the wood.
As we return home,
We see a silver sliver of a moon,
As a ghost-white barn owl,
Glides silently over a silvern field.

The Barn Owl

It is the wing I see first,
Illuminated gold by the early morning sun.
I have heard its startled shrieks at night,
As it surveys the gardens for tasty morsels,
But I haven't seen it before.
Yet here it is
Gliding phantom-like over next-door's garden.
In a flash of brilliant white and gold, it is gone
As if it is a vision or a half-remembered dream.

The Golden Cloak

The low Winter sun spreads its golden cloak,
Over the landscape,
Illuminating the leafless slender trees,
Shining through the wispiness
Of last year's rosebay willowherb.
It could be Spring,
But the biting Arctic wind,
And the frozen ground
Sparkling in the sun
Remind me that we are not there yet.
Jack Frost will play his Winter tricks,
For several more weeks
Before the first primroses are seen
On quiet country lanes
And Lent lillies
Nod their pretty yellow bonnets,
In the March breeze.
But for now, I smile at the sun
And dream of warmer days.

The Mirage

For days the wood has been
Bathed in a golden light,
But today it is smothered,
In a cold silver fog.
As I approach I see the ghostly trees.
The wood is like a faded black-and-white photograph,
Found in the back of a drawer.
Bejewelled silken spiders' webs,
Hang like bunting,
Between last year's hogweed.
Their frost-frozen flower heads
Look as if they are covered,
In ice-cold icing.
Despite our multiple layers
The cold penetrates our bones,
And pinches at our faces.
The ground is hard.
The air is still.
The wood is silent,
Even the birds are cold.
However, as we emerge from the wood,
We see the higher copse,
Which hugs the top of the hill.
It is like a pastel-coloured mirage.

There is light- not much-- but enough,
To add a touch of pink to the clouds
Just above the trees' golden crowns.
The sky is the palest blue,
Enough to make a sailor a hankie.
The new crops in the field
Are the freshest, brightest green.
We stand undecided between the two images.
Looking behind me I see a weak sun,
Hidden behind a silver screen.
The grey trees
Stand still and rigid.
In front of me is the slightest hint of Spring.
Reluctantly, we turn the corner,
And our breath is taken by the Arctic cold.
We trudge homeward.
But I know the light will return.
The warmth will come again.

The Sorcerer's Spell

The wood is bathed in the early morning light.
All is silver, all is still,
Except for the edge of the wood
Which has a golden spotlight,
Shining down onto it,
Illuminating the graceful birches
Turning their trunks from silver to gold.
In that part of the wood the birds sing,
But elsewhere in the forest
There is silence,
Not even the magpies are awake.
The wood is in a dreamlike- state,
Waiting for the golden Winter sun
To release it from the sorcerer's spell.

Teardrops

The trees have been crying.
Teardrops hang from every branch.
Green moss grows on their tear-stained trunks.
Even the air around them is wet with tears.
The sight of it makes me want to weep too,
For the death I know is soon to come,
For the loneliness it will bring,
But then I see a chink of Winter sun
Trying to emerge from the iron-grey sky.
It eventually breaks through,
Bathing the wood and me
In a golden light.
I start to feel better.
You'll soon be gone,
But for now, you're still here,
By my side, looking lovingly at me.
I must not waste this precious time together,
Being sad about what's to come.
Today won't come again,
So I need to savour every second.
The trees seem happier too.
As the sunlight dries their tears,
I stop and try and capture every detail.
You stop too and look at me expectantly.
I stroke your head,

And reassure myself you're still there.
Then off we go,
You and me
Side by side.
The trees will weep again,
And so will I,
But not today.

Birch Ballerinas

The birch trees,
Slender trunks as pale as a swan's neck,
Filigree branches, burnished bronze,
By the early Winter sun,
Stand together like ballerinas waiting to perform.
The breeze stirs the trees,
And they dance together in unison,
As blackbirds and robins sing a chorus.
A squirrel jetes between trees,
But the elegant birches are centre stage,
They are the stars of the show.
They gracefully shake and sway,
It sounds as if their branches are covered,
In tiny silver bells.
They reach a crescendo.
Then the performance is over.
The birch trees take their bow.
All is still again.

Drama in the Sky

I hear the mewing overhead,
And look up.
I see its ragged outline,
Against the cloudless sky.
I watch as it circles on the thermals,
Higher and higher.
It's a peaceful scene until –
First one crow, then two
Appear from nowhere.
They caw loudly.
Angrily, they bombard the buzzard.
Bewildered, it tries to get away,
But they relentlessly pursue him,
Across the bright blue sky.
The buzzard tries to defend himself,
But the crows, who are inexplicably furious,
Take it in turns to dive bomb the buzzard,
Who is acrobatically avoiding them.
They are causing a commotion.
I am surprised there are not more people,
Peering anxiously into the sky,
Hoping the buzzard gets away,
But people are busying by,
Preoccupied by screens or schedules,
Not noticing the drama above their heads.

Finally, the buzzard breaks free,
And hurriedly flies away.
The crows do not want to admit defeat.
They fly around raucously,
Trying to style it out,
Pretending they weren't interested,
In the timid buzzard,
Before nonchalantly idling away.
I go on my way,
Wondering what other dramas
I might see today,
As others hurry unseeingly by.

Jack Frost

Jack Frost has been in the night,
And touched every branch, needle, and leaf.
The wood is white against the dove-grey sky,
It is as if I have gone through the wardrobe,
Into Narnia.
Everything is white.
Last year's hogweed looks like they have been dipped,
In Nitrogen.
And yet if I look carefully I can see colour.
Rose hips rigid and red.
The Robin Hood- green moss clinging to a terracotta trunk.
Wine-coloured alder cones.
And the daffodil -yellow beak of the blackbird,
Singing amongst the lemon-yellow catkins.

The Gale

As light fades,
The wind gets up.
Ghostly trees creak and groan
Like stately galleons
Rounding Cape Horn,
As last year's oak leaves
Skip and twirl and dance
Around my feet.
They look like brown frogs,
Hopping around
And I have to hop, dance and skip,
To avoid them.
They sound like tiny bells,
Dancing down the stairs.
The wind tugs at my hair
And pinches my face.
Our walk is quicker than normal.
We are blown around the park.
As we head home
The wind is in our faces,
Taking my breath away
Almost blowing you over.
The wind roars and howls.
I struggle to open the door,
And we are blown over the threshold.

Then the door is closed.
Calmness returns,
Except for the North wind
Howling angrily down the chimney.

The Young Stag

He appears on the brow of the hill,
Velvet-coated antlers
And cloven hooves.
He looks at me,
Nervously twitching his ear.
I stand still and keep quiet.
He sniffs the air,
And decides what to do next,
Fight or flight?
He chooses flight,
And quickly canters off,
Without a backward glance.
Leaving me on my own
Under the ancient oak tree.

The Trees are Weeping

The trees are weeping," she says,
"An' I have wept plenty of times an' all."
She tells me tales of hunger, poverty, violence,
and fear,
But then aged ten, she did her tasks one day,
Then opened the door and started walking.
She walked to a wild area by the Humber.
It became her refuge, her safe space.
Whilst there she dreamed of another life
Of other rivers she wanted to see,
And other lands across the cold grey North sea,
Which she hoped, one day, to explore.
The daydreams became reality.
She joined the forces and escaped her old life,
But she kept on walking.
When her husband bullied her,
She would go for a walk,
Until the day she walked out on him,
And did not return.
Her walks got longer and longer.
She walked up mountains and across deserts.
She walked so far that her heart went haywire,
But even a pacemaker did not stop her from
walking.

When her second husband died she kept on walking.
"It beats staring at four walls with no one to talk to," she says,
"When I am dead they'll have a helluva job getting the lid on the coffin,
Because my legs will still be moving."
With that, she smiles and says goodbye.
I watch her walk away,
Continuing her walk through life.
There's one final destination,
But she still has many more miles to go.

Magpies

They sit in groups at the top of the trees,
Chattering and gossiping about their neighbours,
Sharing secrets and hatching plots.
They laugh raucously as we pass by,
And I wonder if they are laughing at us.
They fly around the wood,
Their long blue-green tails
Fanning out behind them,
As they spread salacious tittle-tattle,
And keep a watchful eye on all who pass by.

The Brightest Star

Where has the time gone,
Since you walked into my life eleven years ago
And stole my heart?
Back then our life together spread out forever.
I thought about all the places we could explore,
All the experiences we would share.
Our moon was full and bright,
But now it is on the wane.
Your life is near its end.
Soon I will visit our favourite places without
you.
You will not be beside me on the sofa
Or behind me on a walk.
I will have my photographs,
And my memories,
But you'll be gone.
As I cry for you
Every night I will look up at you,
The brightest star in the sky.

The Swan

It emerges from the misty lake,
Elegant neck extended
Angelic arms outstretched.
It skims across the water
Then ascends slowly
Into the chaffinch-pink sky.
I see it gradually disappear.
It doesn't leave a trace,
Not a ripple or snowflake feather.
Only I know it has been here,
Only I know that you are here too.

Dawn Chorus

As dawn breaks
The bird chorus gets louder.
The tits and finches are raucously and hysterically,
Twittering in the birch trees by the wetland,
Whilst a wren, his song is as clear as a young Aled Jones,
Tries to get them back on track.
Then the rooks, magpies, and jackdaws join in.
They are like drunk friends at a karaoke,
Thinking they are Beyonce.
There's lots of enthusiasm, but no tune.
Thank goodness for the robins and blackbirds,
Singing the mellifluous melodies,
As the sun slowly rises.
The avian choral symphony
Reaches an alarming crescendo,
And then everyone gives up, exhausted,
Apart from the solo song of a blackbird
As the golden light
Spreads across the wood.

The Lane

We take a different route today,
Along the lane,
Overlooked by the chalk-white hill–horse,
Not ancient, but old.
To the West, fertile fields spread towards,
Distant dusky dales.
Ancient oak and ash, like gnarled giants,
Stand, dominantly, across the landscape.
From the wood to our East,
There's a cacophony of birdsong.
This is an old lane,
Used by packhorses and drovers long ago,
And now our feet tread here.
Soon, others will come this way too,
But for now, it's just you and me.

One Colour at a Time

The wood is yellow this morning,
Primrose-yellow catkins against the
sapphire-blue sky,
Lemony- lichen on the slender trees,
Vivid yellow staghorn on the mossy stump,
The buttermilk-yellow underside of the buzzard
As it glides across the sky above me.
The dark yellow fresh buds of the sycamore,
The flash of yellow on a goldfinch's wing.
Spring is coming, I think,
One colour at a time.
First comes the yellow,
Then the pale pink apple blossom,
The crimson tulips in the garden,
The violets in the hedge backs,
The ink-blue bluebells in the ancient wood,
The bright new green leaves on the blackthorn,
The copper-orange Comma.
One colour at a time,
The landscape is changing,
Spring is returning.

By the light of the Silver Moon

I am walking through the silent wood.
My way is lit up by the silvern moon.
My hair is like burnished gold.
I wear a silken cloak, which glitters
In the light of the full moon.
I feel the crunch of last year's leaves
Underneath my cold, bare feet.
I am searching for something,
But I can't remember what it is I seek,
Only that I must find it here.
Then I see you in the moonlight.
As our fingers touch we turn to stardust
And dance by the light of the silver moon.

www.ingramcontent.com/pod-product-compliance
Lightning Source LLC
Chambersburg PA
CBHW051754130826
49812CB00033B/1140
9789357442985